To: Courtney

From: Nick

COMPENDIUM®
live inspired

With special thanks to the entire Compendium family.

CREDITS:
Written by: Danielle Leduc
Illustrated by: Jill Tytherleigh
Designed by: Sarah Forster
Edited by: Ruth Austin

Library of Congress Control Number: 2016945338
ISBN: 978-1-943200-36-8

2nd printing. Printed in China with soy inks on FSC©-certified paper.

***

because you're the

ABSOLUTE
BEST

***

The following is a concise,
but by no means exhaustive,
list of things I would do for you:

———

Eat spiders.

———

Listen to dubstep.
Fight Jackie Chan.

I'd buy you a hundred kittens,

and clean the kitty litter
for a hundred kittens.

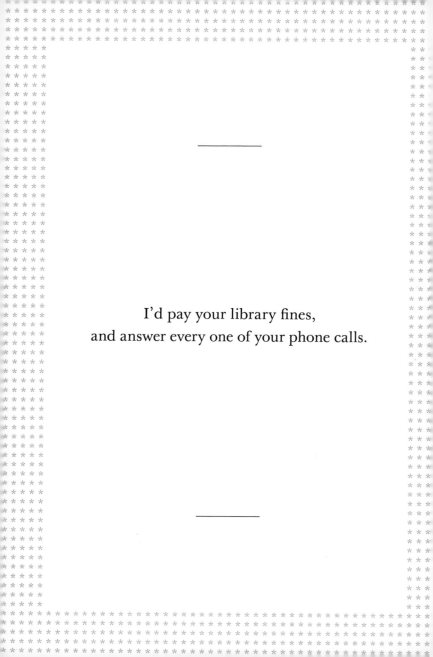

I'd pay your library fines,
and answer every one of your phone calls.

———————

I'd lean out the window
of the world's tallest building

———————

to give you a wave.

I would even move to Saskatchewan.

If it came to it,

—————

I'd break you out of prison
using only a nail file,
night vision goggles,

—————

_____

and a lock-picking hamster.

_____

If you went missing, I'd become a private eye.

I'd assemble a wily team of experts
who would work around the clock
to bring you home.

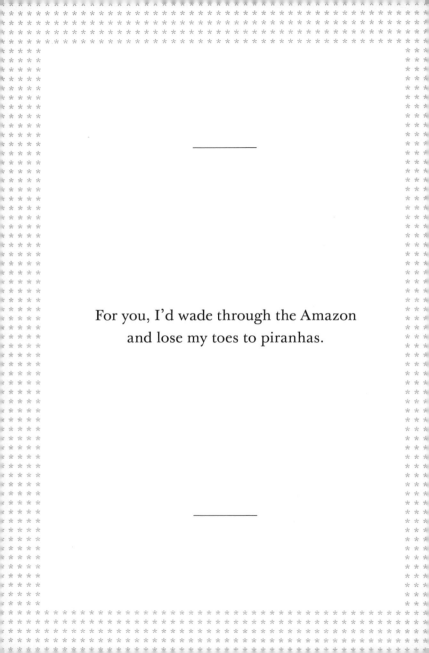

For you, I'd wade through the Amazon
and lose my toes to piranhas.

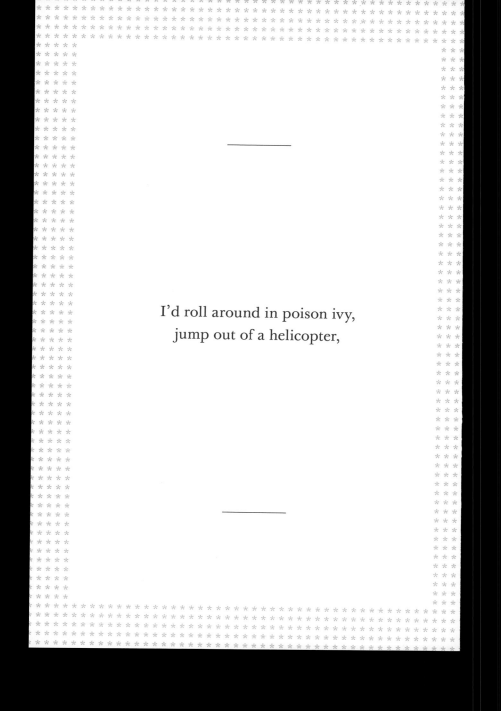

————

I'd roll around in poison ivy,
jump out of a helicopter,

————

———

and run into a burning building
to save you, your high school poetry,
and every snack in your cupboard.

———

———————

If it made you happy,
I'd watch daytime TV with you,

———————

—————

and wear tear-away pants

—————

for the rest of my life.

I'd eat every hot dog on earth.
Without ketchup. Just... dry.

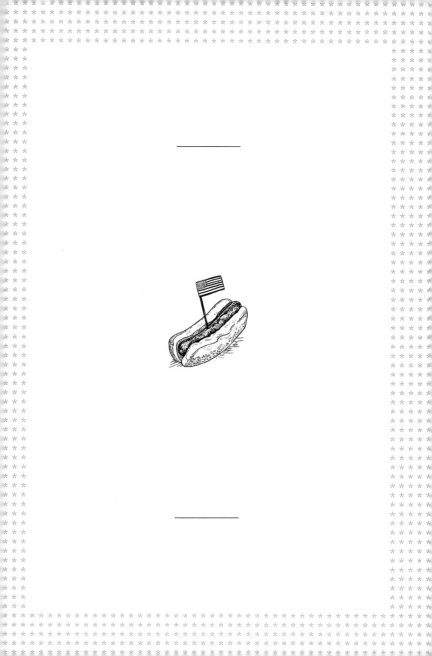

I'd give you the last cookie.

I'd even wear toe socks.

_____

If I could,

_____

———

I'd invent a new ice cream flavor for you,
made from the golden skins of perfectly
toasted marshmallows.

———

I'd send you back in time to inspire
the Beatles to write every song about you
(except the sad ones).

If you needed me to,
I'd drive you across state lines
and not ask any questions.

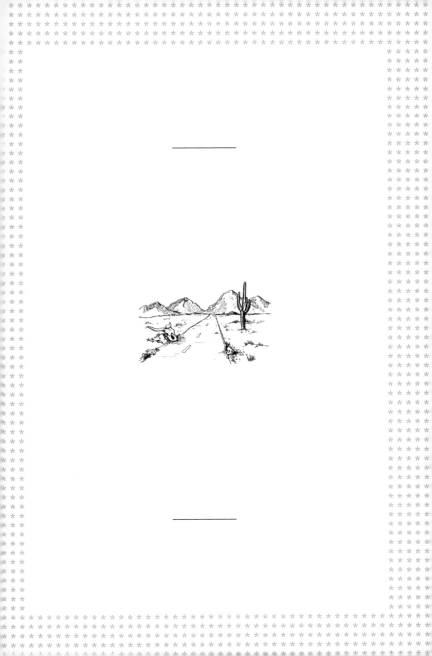

I'd dine alfresco in the Arctic,
let you have the window seat,
belly flop from a high dive,

and save you from a giant squid.

I'd push through the thorniest thickets
to fetch you the plumpest blackberries.

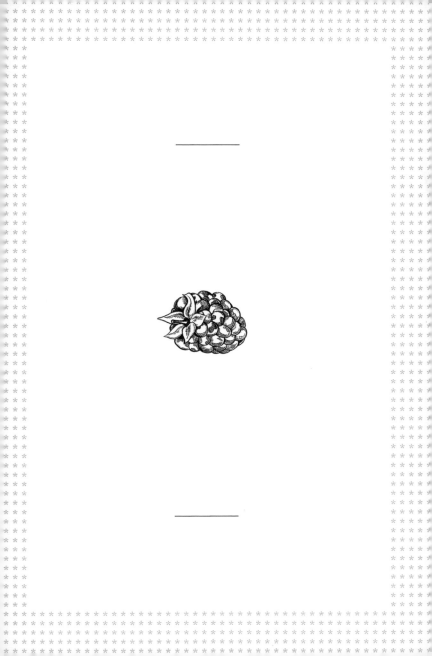

I'd bake you a lifetime supply of pies,

and help you eat a lifetime supply of pies.

I'd invent a happiness machine for you,
and not even try to patent it.

I'd give you everything I've got,
tell you the words you need to hear,

and listen to all of the secrets, fears,
hopes, and ideas hiding in your brain.

I'd do all of these things and more,

because

———

you're a category five storm of awesome,

———

a galaxy of cool,
and an outright phenomenon!

You're not just the best,
but the *absolute* best.

...please don't make me eat spiders.